IGNORE THAT
BUZZ

*Identify, understand and tackle digital
distractions to become more productive*

Ramanathan J

Cover designed by Ramanathan J

CONTENTS

INTRODUCTION

We are living in a world of unprecedented connectivity. We can access the internet from our smartphones, laptops and desktop computers. We can use voice enabled assistant devices such as Alexa to search for information or to order products online. We receive countless notifications on our smartphones whenever our friends message us on WhatsApp or other similar instant messaging platforms.

However, we often wonder whether we are empowered or distracted by the state of constant digital connectivity. We may try to focus on a task before we are distracted by a new social media feed on an app or a browser tab. We would think of taking one quick look at the new WhatsApp forward or a funny meme on Facebook before returning to our task. Later, we realize that we have spent nearly two hours mindlessly scrolling up and down the browser or chat windows.

It is time that we become self-aware of our schedules and priorities amidst the constant barrage of digital information that we face on a daily basis. We must stop treating our digital gadgets as necessary companions. Instead, we must start considering our devices as inlets of digital information over whom we have absolute control.

This brief guide will enable you to detect and modify your own behavioral patterns when it comes to interaction with technology. This guide will empower you to substitute your reflexive response to technology with healthier alternatives. Removing addiction like dependency on technology will create more time for yourself that you can use to spend quality time with your family or to achieve your personal goals. Finally, a distraction free environment will allow you to complete complex or challenging tasks with a laser like focus.

I will focus on the prime culprits who create relentless distraction and will provide simple strategies for countering these interruptions. You would need to understand the underlying mechanisms that cause the interruptions and become alert enough to stop reacting instinctively to these distractions. The eventual objective of the entire exercise is to remove the dependency on these apps as a source to fulfil a temporary excitement or rush.

Your goals for handling these distractions will be complete when you are able to move beyond or ignore these distractions. You can declare yourself as free from digital distractions when you no longer use your digital devices such as smartphones or laptops primarily for entertainment. Instead, you use these devices only for transactional or commercial purposes.

Anatomy of a distraction

What is one of the first activities that we perform when we wake up in the morning? We pick up a toothbrush, put some toothpaste on it and start brushing. We do not have to put any conscious thought to the entire process. The whole act of brushing after waking up is like a muscle memory or a reflex action to us.

What is your first reaction when you hear a notification sound from your smartphone? What do you do when you see the tiny light, which indicates new message or notification, blinking at the top of your smartphone? Think about your responses to the above questions for a moment before you proceed further.

Chances are you would instinctively take your smartphone, unlock the screen and tap on the message notification to check further details. You would have accomplished all of this in a few seconds time. A part of our muscle memory now includes our response to a new message notification sound or a blinking light.

You might wonder how reacting to a smartphone message notification has become an impulsive or a reflex activity for many people. What makes people to pick up their phones and check for new messages whenever they see a new message notification irrespective of whether they are commuting to work or whether they are working on an important task in their workplace?

Social media giants and companies that develop the popular smartphone apps have one objective- to increase user engagement with the app. More users using the app for a longer time would make the app more popular and would create more data for companies to analyze the user behavior. Companies rely on the way human beings form habits to create new habits among consumers for frequently using their apps.

Charles Duhigg has explained the fascinating process by which humans form new habits in his remarkable book titled "The Power of Habit: Why We Do What We Do in Life and Business". If we interpret the theory mentioned in the book, we can conclude that human beings experience the following stages in a linear manner before they complete any task or activity as a part of their habit:

Any human being, irrespective of the complexity of the activity he/she is about to accomplish, will experience these four stages. When a consumer goes through these four stages on a constant basis while using a product or service, then that consumer will soon form a habit for the brand.

Cue is a multi-sensory trigger that an individual could experience at any moment. Cue or a trigger can be visual, auditory or taste based. Even time of the day could activate a cue. Cue forms the basis for experiencing further tasks of any habit. For example, assume that you are in your workplace and you look at your watch few hours after lunch. You find that the time is 3 PM. You leave your workstation and head to the nearest coffee machine to drink a cup of coffee.

Now, assume that you are driving home from your workplace and you see the bright neon sign of the pizza restaurant in the neighborhood. Chances are that the cue for your habit of eating pizza could be the brightly lit signboard. Similarly, you might smell the freshly baked pizzas when you walk by the restaurant. In this case, your cue for eating pizza is the smell of fresh pizzas. Thus, cue is the initial sensory trigger that sets an individual on the path of completing an activity or a task as a part of habit.

Cue does not directly lead to action on the part of an individual. Instead, an individual initially experiences craving for reward in an intermediate stage. Thus, you might look at the signboard of a pizza restaurant while driving home and immediately you may experience a yearning for eating pizza. The craving for reward in this case is to feel the taste of freshly baked pizzas.

However, we may not immediately realize or understand the reward that we really seek. It may seem that we crave for one reward on the surface. However, in reality, we might be fulfilling our desire for some other experience by obtaining this reward. For instance, you are in your workplace and you look at the time few hours after lunch. You realize that it is 3 PM and you grab a cup of coffee from a vending machine nearby.

You may think that the craving for reward is to gain energy and remove drowsiness by drinking a cup of coffee. However, the real craving in this case could be to remove boredom by engaging in social interaction that you can experience while drinking coffee and chatting with your colleagues. Thus, identifying the real reward that you seek from a habit is crucial in decoding your behavioral patterns.

Digital distractions are also deeply entrenched habits. We need to understand the underlying reward that we seek from these digital distractions before we can address them.

How does digital distraction
affect our productivity?

You may be now wondering why digital distraction is such an important issue. You may think how browsing Facebook for couple of minutes or looking at few chats and responding to few of them on WhatsApp would affect the efficiency or productivity of an individual.

You might reason that we drink coffee couple of times in a day in our workplaces. You may debate that we walk by to nearby workstations many times in a day to have a light-hearted chat with our colleagues or friends. The question is how these activities are different from attending to a digital distraction.

We can perform some of our daily activities such as brushing our teeth or eating our breakfast naturally or easily. We do not need to think about what to do next when it comes to performing these activities. It is as if these activities are a part of our muscle memory.

On the other hand, when we send an email to someone or when we reply to a chat message, we need to think at least for a moment before we compose our response. Even when we look at our friends' pictures uploaded on Facebook or forwarded on WhatsApp, we need to pause and think about the picture for a moment.

We need to think about various aspects of a photograph such as when did my friend took this picture, where did my friend take this picture, what is he/she wearing in the picture, who else are present in the picture and so on. Thus, any interaction with a digital device or app requires at least a minimal amount of cognitive thinking.

We have limited willpower and cognitive energy reserves that we use for completing our tasks in a day. When we perform any simple activity such as drinking a cup of coffee or talking to our friends in person, we use very little cognitive energy reserves or willpower.

However, when we try to complete a relatively complex activity such as playing a game of chess or drafting an email in a limited time, we spend a significant amount of our crucial energy reserves and willpower. When we focus a lot on digital distractions such as WhatsApp or Facebook, we constantly spend our cognitive energy reserves to understand the various pictures posted on social media, to think, and to type responses to various chats or comments.

When we go back to our workplace tasks that are to be on priority, we need to spend more of our limited willpower to focus on our tasks. This is to ensure that the next status update on Facebook or the latest chat on WhatsApp does not distract us from finally focus on our high priority tasks.

However, when we drink a cup of coffee from the vending machine or socialize with our colleagues or friends at our workplace, we need not spend enough of our cognitive energy reserves to attend to these interruptions.

Similarly, when we return to our work after drinking coffee or after having a light-hearted conversation with our friends, we need not spend enough of our willpower to focus again on our tasks. Hence, a well-timed coffee break or casual conversation with friends does not affect our productivity as adversely as checking WhatsApp or Facebook frequently.

DIGITAL DISTRACTION: INSTANT MESSAGING APPS

Imagine this for a moment. You are about to work on a very important task. You have written your notes regarding the activity. You are deep in thought trying to figure out a solution. Then when you are about to try a possible solution for the task, you hear a new message notification sound on your smartphone.

You unlock your smartphone, pull down the menu, tap on the notification and then you arrive on the screen of an instant messaging app (e.g. WhatsApp). Your friend has forwarded you a funny meme that he has seen on a social media platform. You respond with your comment on the meme.

You see two grey colored ticks appearing next to the message moments after you send it. You occasionally look at the grey ticks. Soon, the grey color changes to blue. It means that your friend has read the message. Meanwhile, you go to the home screen of the messaging app. Some of your other friends have send you couple of messages as well. You look at these messages and start responding to them.

When you finally place your phone down, you realize that you have been browsing through messages for the past 20 minutes. You take a while to trace your original train of thought regarding the complex task that you were supposed to work on a while back.

Although you were able to trace some of your initial ideas about the task, you are now unable to maintain focus on the activity. Your attention and cognitive resources have depleted while responding to the messages on the messaging app. The instant messaging app has successfully distracted you.

Instant messaging apps function to exploit the cue-craving for reward- task- reward behavioral pattern. Message notification sound, blinking light, grey and blue ticks and a simplified user interface work towards making consumer a habitual user of the app. Once you start interacting with the app, you will start seeing responses from various users.

Once you observe the two blue ticks against your sent message, you will understand that your friends have read your message. Soon you will monitor the app frequently anticipating your friend's response to your message. If your friend does not respond to your message, you will then start wondering the reasons for the same.

Is your friend not bothered enough to respond? Is your friend deliberately ignoring your message? Your attention is now fixated on the messaging app. You are now more bothered about who has responded to your messages, who has sent a new joke or funny picture, what is the latest gossip happening in numerous groups. Your priority for other crucial tasks or for personal interaction with friends or family becomes secondary.

In other words, these instant messaging apps make you an addict. The app features are designed in such a way to increase your addiction and craving for the digital platform. So how can we manage to avoid distraction from instant messaging apps?

We need to understand what we gain from tapping on the messaging app frequently. Do we gain social connectivity by interacting with our friends through the app? Do we gain a break from the routine activities at the workplace by looking at the jokes and funny forwards? Does the interaction with app in itself triggers the dopamine rush that we seek so frequently?

We also need to identify the real underlying reason for our interaction with the app. The most commonly stated reason could be that we are using the app to contact our friends. However, the real reason for using the app may not be so obvious.

Some of us may consider the messaging app a primary source of escape. Some may consider the funny forwards and jokes a welcome distraction. Some may feel social isolation even though they may belong to a team in a workplace. Hence, such people may use the messaging app to seek social connectivity. Checking messages and responding to them may be the most preferred means for such individuals to establish social connectivity.

Once we understand the underlying reason for our need to use the instant messaging app frequently, we can identify strategies to prevent this digital distraction. Some of the possible methods to counter this digital distraction are as follows:

1. Call instead of message: Each time when you see the tiny light blinking at the top of your smartphone, do not react by expand the notification and read the message. Instead, go to

your contacts list and randomly call any friend or family member from this list.

You can also get up from your desk, walk to a nearby workstation and speak to your colleague regarding work or some trivial topic such as weather or sports. Soon, you will emerge out of this need to spend time reading and responding to a message every time you listen a notification sound or see a new message indicator.

2. Disable notification sound: You would need to look at the phone in order to see the new message notification blinking light for WhatsApp. However, you can hear the new message notification sound anytime and this can cause distraction. You can prevent this by turning off the new message notification sound in WhatsApp. In this way, you can prevent distractions resulting from new message notifications in WhatsApp.

3. Set expectations: We expect that we will find new excitement every time when we open the

instant messenger app. We hope that we will have great conversations and humorous interactions every time when we send a message to our friends.

Take a look at some of your past chat messages and identify how many of them were humorous, exciting or full of wisdom. Chances are, many of these conversations would have been bland. Many of these conversations would have involved customary greetings, jokes or funny forwards.

You must understand that many chat conversations will be uninteresting. You must also understand that you would still use the messenger app frequently hoping to engage in some interesting conversation soon. Instead of starting the messenger app and hoping to engage in an exciting chat, walk to a nearby colleague or friend and engage in face-to-face conversation occasionally. You can also call a friend outside of your workplace.

When you gradually begin to substitute online conversations with meaningful and in-person interactions, you will realize that it is simply not worth your energy to focus obsessively on messenger chat and gossip.

4. Uninstall the messenger: It may happen that you tried all the strategies listed above and yet the instant messenger app consumes a lot of your free time and distracts you during your work. In that case, you can go ahead and uninstall the app itself. This may look like a radical strategy but in some cases, going cold turkey on the instant messenger may be the best solution.

   You would need to think beyond the instant messenger for social interaction and connectivity once you uninstall the app. You may ask how your friends will communicate with you once you have removed the instant messenger. I would say that you are still available on phone and SMS.

If any of your friend really wishes to contact you, then he/she can take the extra effort to dial your number and speak to you over the phone. If your friend thinks that you are worth contacting only through WhatsApp messages and does not bother to call you, then perhaps you need to think whether such an individual is a real friend or is just an online acquaintance.

If it is the latter case, then you anyways do not need instant messenger for shallow and superficial conversations. You can now focus more on phone and in person interactions and strive towards making these conversations more fruitful, fulfilling and interesting.

DIGITAL DISTRACTION: FACEBOOK APP

Facebook app is a digital distraction that can easily capture your attention and energy. Although you might spend couple of minutes going through new status updates, quotes and pictures on Facebook, you would keep thinking about the posts long after you have exited the app. You might even spend more time on the app if you are commuting to work or returning home. You would often "like" posts and comment on some of them. You could also upload your selfie or create a famous quote post on your Facebook "wall". Subsequently, you would look at your own posts to check for number of likes and comments.

We need to understand what Facebook offers and why we need to use the app frequently. Facebook defines itself as a social media platform for connecting to friends and family relatives. Facebook also projects itself as a simpler means for interacting and sharing content with friends and family. Many users also mention that they were able to find their former colleagues from school and college on the website.

The question that now arises is as to whether there are any other alternatives to contact our friends and relatives besides posting and commenting on Facebook. You can send an email to our friends. You can also open the contact list on your phone and call your friends or relatives. In case you are unaware of some of your friends' latest contact numbers and/or email IDs, you can call some mutual friend and try to obtain updated contact details. Instead, why do you prefer to scroll up and down on Facebook to look at walls, posts and pictures uploaded by your friends and relatives?

Here is an exercise that you can try. Identify how many of your friends and relatives on Facebook have spoken to you over the phone or have met you in-person recently? Chances are that many of these friends and relatives are content in interacting with you just on Facebook. The preferred way for these friends and relatives to contact you could be to post likes and comments on your Facebook wall.

Now we face a possible paradox. Your friends are keen to share their photos and status updates on their Facebook wall. However, they are also equally reluctant to pick up their phones to call you or to meet you in person.

This could imply one possible reason. Facebook is a platform for narcissistic haves and aspiring have-nots. Facebook brings out the worst of attention seeking and self-boasting behavior among individuals. If your friend has visited an exotic foreign location for a vacation with his/her spouse, then he/she will upload the vacation pictures on Facebook. He/she will probably crave for likes and comments on those vacation pictures. Your friend might also upload pictures of him/her having a great time at a restaurant or a pub.

Narcissistic haves will flaunt their achievements and trophies on Facebook. Aspiring have-nots will look at these posts and will yearn for such trophies or will agonize at the lack of it. Aspiring have-nots may also try to compete by posting their own trophies that may seem relatively trivial compared to those of the narcissistic counterparts.
The aspiring have-nots hope to have their own share of likes and comments. Soon the whole activity of looking at Facebook wall, liking, commenting and uploading own posts as well as pictures turns into a relentless game of digital one-upmanship.

You need to ask yourself whether you intend to be a part of this digital popularity contest that happens daily on Facebook. You need to ask yourself whether you want to be associated with a phenomenon in which you build and maintain your digital brand by constantly seeking social approval.

I would say that Facebook is a tremendous digital distraction. You are not only distracted whenever you start the app and go through the posts but also long after you have exited the app. Your mind replays the pompous pictures and status updates of narcissistic haves. Instead of focusing on the task that is to be completed, you think about the drama of social media prima donnas and attention seekers that unfolds daily on Facebook.

The only strategy to deal with this digital distraction resulting from Facebook is to delete the account and to uninstall the app. There is no moderation when it comes to Facebook. Either you can remain obsessed with the platform and all the inherent shenanigans or you can remove the app and focus on utilizing your energy in a productive manner.

You may wonder that your friends and relatives will not be too pleased if you decide to delete your Facebook account. Chances are nobody is too bothered about whether you retain your Facebook account or whether you delete it. You can just call or mail your friends and mention that you would not be available on

Facebook because of other priorities and that they can either call or email you in case they wish to contact you.

If you have successfully deleted your Facebook account and you are feeling compelled to check on the latest social media gossip and updates among your friends, you can just choose a friend's number randomly from your contact list and call him/her.

You can purchase a greeting card, write few thoughtful lines on it and send it to your friend or relative. They will be surprised and pleased by the effort you took to send a card. You can also write a long letter and initiate a meaningful conversation.

In this way, you will come to know about which of your friends are willing to go beyond the shallow interactions on the social media and are interested to engage in genuine and lasting relationships.

If you stop hearing from your friends after you have deleted your Facebook account, then maybe those friends of yours were mere social media acquaintances and perhaps it is better to think beyond these contacts and move on.

DIGITAL DISTRACTION: TWITTER

Twitter has become the most preferred platform for celebrities, politicians, sportspersons and almost anyone to express their opinions on any subject. Organizations and government departments have their official Twitter "handles" that they use to provide updates or new developments in their area of work. News channels and papers also use the platform to provide the latest breaking news.

However, Twitter is infamous for another phenomenon – debates and arguments. It seems that every third tweet is some individual debating in favor of or against some topic or ideology. A new hashtag (any term or phrase preceded by # sign) trends on Twitter every hour and day. Many of these hashtags relate to some politician or breaking news.

All you need to do to join the ongoing debate is to use the hashtag term and write your own opinion on the subject. As soon as you post the tweet, it will be available on the global platform. Soon, other users will retweet, like your tweet or will reply to your tweet. If your tweet is more popular, your tweet will get more number of retweets and likes.

All the tweets that you post is also available on your own Twitter timeline. Your Twitter timeline is like your profile page and is similar to the Facebook wall. You can follow other Twitter users and you can receive updates from these users on your timeline. Many people on Twitter follow politicians, film celebrities, sports icons and organizations.

Similarly, other users can also follow you on Twitter. A user with large number of followers on Twitter is indeed popular. Such popular users are also opinion influencers since they can broadcast their views on any topic quickly to their large number of followers.

Twitter is also full of trolls or anonymous accounts, who stalk, criticize and make fun of other popular users. Trolls could belong to both sides of views or political ideologies. Trolls are also the source of funny memes, witty images and snarky retorts.

When a user signs up for a new account on Twitter, he/she can attain various objectives by using the platform. The user can use his/her real name and identity to create a new Twitter account. Such user could intend to voice his opinions on various topics and he has no qualms about using his real identity for doing so.

Another type of user could create an anonymous account on Twitter. He/she could use this anonymous account to act as a troll. Such users could use their Twitter accounts to stalk, criticize or make fun of prominent personalities or opposing ideologies.

Finally, we can also see the fan follower type of accounts on Twitter. These users are not interested to engage in political discussions. Instead, such users follow their favorite celebrities or sports icons to update themselves on the latest status updates or pictures of their stars.

Twitter hooks its users by unleashing a barrage of content at them the moment they open the social media site. You can see your tweets, the number of likes and retweets for your tweets, the posts of those whom you follow, and a list of hashtags and phrases that are trending worldwide in a simple and clutter free screen.

You need to figure out your objectives for using Twitter. Do you use the platform to play mischief on other prominent users? Do you like to use Twitter to get the latest breaking news from across the globe? Do you like to follow your favorite celebrity on the social media platform?

You need to understand that you will visit Twitter for fulfilling one objective and will stay on the site for longer duration for other reasons. For example, you will think of going to twitter website or app to check your timeline for a few minutes. You read a few tweets from your favorite celebrity who you follow.

Meanwhile, you see an interesting hashtag that is trending globally. You click on the hashtag link and see thousands of tweets related to the topic. You browse through these tweets and notice one particular tweet with a large number of retweets and likes. You click on this tweet and find some other interesting tweets in reply screen.

You soon realize that you have spent an hour reading various tweets whereas you had initially planned to spend only few minutes on Twitter.

Twitter will unleash content from various users on a variety of topics the moment you open the site or app. This platform can be a huge digital distraction unless you plan your response. You can deal with this digital distraction by applying any of the following techniques:

1. Allot time: Allocate a specific time either in afternoon or in evening to browse through your

Twitter timeline. Do not allocate time to view your Twitter timeline in the morning because this will distract your attention even before you commence your tasks. Follow this schedule and ensure that you visit the Twitter website or app only during the allotted time.

2. Limit to following news handles: If you find the content overload on Twitter to be overwhelming, you can restrict Twitter for just checking the latest news. Unfollow celebrity handles, political observers, funny trolls and other Twitter handles who will lead you down the rabbit hole of memes, witty posts and funny videos.

3. Uninstall the app: You can find alternative sources of information if you want news updates. You can go to a news website or an app and find latest breaking news. You can also just read a newspaper copy the next day. In case you use Twitter to follow celebrities, you can analyze whether it is worth to attend to a digital distraction just to keep track of minute-to-minute updates of celebrities and sports icons.

Like Facebook, you can simply uninstall the app and move on to spend your time in a quality manner elsewhere.

DIGITAL DISTRACTION: YOUTUBE

We can upload and view videos on YouTube. Individual users can use their Google accounts to create their own "channels" on YouTube. Other users can view this content and can then choose to subscribe to the channel. Thus, more popular the content on any channel, more the number of subscribers the channel may have.

YouTube is similar to twitter while presenting content to users. YouTube displays a plethora of videos from various genres or categories whenever users open the website. User may have opened YouTube to watch a specific content but when he views the front page of the website, he will find videos from other interesting categories. As a result, he would view one recommended video after another for an extended duration of time.

You can watch videos on any topic that you may have in your mind. Individuals, movie studios as well as television networks all have their own channels on YouTube. Content creators always strive to attract and retain more subscribers. Thus, video uploaders create more content in any specific category whereas viewers have a huge number of videos to watch.

When you go to YouTube, you have an almost unlimited number of videos to watch from multiple categories. Like a cable television with thousands of channels, you can browse from one video to another until you start watching a specific content.

If you think that you will go to YouTube and casually search for some videos, you are most likely going to spend a lot of time aimlessly wandering through various channels and videos. Hence, YouTube can be a formidable digital distraction that can easily lure in unsuspecting viewers. You can spend hours to browse various channels and to watch one video after another.

Before you begin to tackle YouTube as a digital distraction, you need to determine your objectives for visiting the website. You may visit YouTube to watch videos about a specific subject that you are currently learning on your own. You may visit YouTube to listen to music in background while you are engaged in other tasks. You could also visit YouTube for just entertainment.

It may also happen that you open YouTube with the objective of learning something new about a subject. However, you view a "recommended" video thumbnail and you are distracted within the website itself. You click on this recommended video and you see some thumbnails of other interesting videos.

You open the website with a specific objective, for instance to watch educational content or to listen to background music. However, you stayed on the website for a different reason, i.e. entertainment. You are also distracted from other tasks that were to be completed.

Thus, you can handle YouTube as a digital distraction in the following manner:

1. Allocate time: You can allocate specific time slots in a day when you would access YouTube. As we saw in case of Twitter, you can allot time slots in afternoon or evening for accessing YouTube. You must not identify time slots for browsing YouTube in the morning because this will distract your attention before you even start your tasks. You can preferably access YouTube later in the day by when you would have completed a substantial portion of your tasks.

2. Visit specific channels: If you intend to access YouTube for specific purpose such as to learn more about a new subject or to listen to music in background while you focus on other activities, then you can note down the URLs or links of these YouTube channels. Next time when you want to visit YouTube, you can directly access these channels by their links that you stored earlier. In this way, recommended video thumbnails would not distract you when you can directly access the specific content that is available in related YouTube channels.

3. Seek alternatives: You need not consider YouTube the only source for the content that you seek. If you are seeking educational videos, you can visit other online education content providers such as edx.org or Coursera. Edx.org has many self-paced training programs on a variety of subjects that are free of cost. Similarly, if you seek background music that can help, you focus on your task; you can visit sites such as Spotify or tunein.com and choose streaming music that can help you focus.

YouTube is a very effective digital distraction because it has a predominant video and audio content. Browsing YouTube is like surfing hundreds of channels on a cable television. Your mind seeks distraction and excitement. YouTube has numerous films, songs, gameplay videos and other content that can engage you for hours at a stretch.

You should have an objective in terms of specific content or channel before you access YouTube. If you intend to access YouTube casually or without any specific goal, you must do so in an allotted time after you have completed a substantial portion of your day's tasks. It would also be preferable if you can find the content that you are seeking in other sources or websites.

DIGITAL DISTRACTION: GAMES

Gaming represents a multibillion-dollar industry worldwide. Games can work in computers, smartphones or dedicated consoles such as PlayStation or Xbox. Games can belong to various categories such as action, adventure, sports, strategy, fantasy, simulation, role-playing and so on.

Computer games that were initially developed were simplified and pixelated software that offered little gameplay value. However, recent gaming titles provide highly realistic graphical detail along with enormous gameplay value.

Games have an enormous distraction value. The rich playing experience provides enough incentive for players to distract from their other tasks. Some games have a feature called as open world role-playing capability that allows the players to explore a vast virtual world in various roles. This allows players countless hours of gameplay value. Many players have spent thousands of hours in such games trying to explore every corner of the virtual world.

Some gaming experience can grab complete attention of players. This gameplay experience can be so enthralling that players can completely ignore other aspects of their lives such as hunger, thirst, sleep and work.

We need to identify gaming as a digital distraction and not a leisurely pastime. We can tackle digital distraction in the form of gaming by applying the following strategies:

1. Uninstall gaming apps from smartphone: You can do away with the numerous gaming apps on

your phone. You need not spend your time trying to win a virtual game while you commute to or from work. Instead, you can listen to music or meditate during your travel. Even if you get bored, you need not constantly seek digital sources of entertainment such as games.

2. Sell your console: If you own a PlayStation or Xbox console, then you can sell it right away. You need not possess a dedicated hardware that can provide you with a source of constant digital distraction.

3. Play real sports: You can start playing real sports such as tennis, soccer or badminton instead of relying on virtual games. You can increase your fitness level and gain energy by playing real sports.

4. Workout or exercise: If you consider games a digital distraction to channel your inner aggression or frustration, then you can substitute such games with exercise or workout. Intense workout or exercise will not only help

you to channel your inner aggression or frustration but also will help you in building your fitness levels as well as energy levels.

As we saw in case of Facebook, there is no scope of moderation with gaming as well. You have limited cognitive reserves that you use for various tasks every day. When you attend to distraction in the form of gaming, you drain your limited energy and cognitive faculties to play and excel in games.

Even if you play games after you complete your day's work, this digital distraction will adversely affect your quality of rest and sleep. Hence, it is better to play real sports or to exercise or workout instead of focusing our attention on computer or smartphone games.

SPECIAL FOCUS: MORNING SCHEDULE

You may think that digital distractions wreak havoc on our productivity only when we access Facebook, WhatsApp etc. while commuting or while working in office. However, early morning is another very important part of your daily schedule.

Your activities and priorities immediately after you wake up in morning sets the tone for the rest of your day. If you check your smartphone for new messages and emails immediately after you wake up in morning, then you would be in a state of digital trance for the rest of the day.

If you prefer to instantly check your latest social media feed and WhatsApp forwards once you wake up, then you would be equally dazed and distracted for the entire day.

How you spend your time immediately after you wake up in the morning sets the tone for the rest of the day? If your immediate priority after waking up is to respond to digital distractions, then you would be looking out for these distractions throughout the day.

Instead, you may choose to meditate or workout after waking up. Meditation or exercise will increase your energy levels. You may even go for a walk or make your own breakfast. These activities need not require any digital intermediary.

Do not start swiping your smartphones once you wake up. The blinking light or notification icon may persuade you to check for new messages and status updates. However, you must steer clear of digital distractions once you wake up.

You can get an alarm clock so that you will not be dependent on your smartphone to set an alarm to wake you in the morning. Thus, may even switch off your smartphone once you are about to sleep. You can switch it on once you leave for work.

You can consider your key priority to build your energy levels in the morning by focusing on activities such as mediation or exercise.

CONCLUSION:

We can access the digital ecosystem through various devices such as smartphones, smart watches, voice enabled assistants, laptops and so on. However, our constant connectivity to the digital world also allows digital distractions to capture our attention. We must be able to identify, understand and tackle each digital distraction separately.

www.ingramcontent.com/pod-product-compliance
Lightning Source LLC
Chambersburg PA
CBHW020331290526
45785CB00007B/3005